Copyright © 2013, 2017
make believe ideas ltd
The Wilderness, Berkhamsted, Hertfordshire, HP4 2AZ, UK.
6th Fl., South Bank House, Barrow St., Dublin 4, D04 TR29, Ireland.

All rights reserved. No part of this publication may be reproduced,
stored in a retrieval system, or transmitted in any form or by any means,
electronic, mechanical, photocopying, recording, or otherwise, or used
to train any artificial intelligence technologies without the
prior written permission of the copyright owner.

www.makebelieveideas.co.uk
enquiries@makebelieveideas.com

Written by Gabrielle Mercer.
Illustrated by Lara Ede.

My very first Prayers

make believe ideas

This is my prayer book
to help me to pray.
I like to read it
each and every day.

You can **pray** when you are **running**, being *still* or **playing** too!

You don't need **long words** – anything will do!

Pray with eyes **closed** or **open**, standing tall or with **head bowed.** You can pray just by **thinking,** or saying words out **loud.**

Thank God for being by your side each second of the day. Thank Him for being your **best friend** and hearing all you want to say.

Tell God **all** your worries,
what makes you happy, 
cross or sad.

Always know that you can
trust Him –
He's your loving   
heavenly Dad.

Let's pray

When things go **well** and we're feeling **happy**, we can say...

Thank you!
God has given us so many **good** things – let's give Him **thanks**.

Praise Him!
God's world is **fantastic**!
It's great to be **alive**!
Let's share our **excitement** with Him.

"Give thanks to the Lord, for he is good; his love endures forever." 1 Chronicles 16:34 (NIV)

When things go **wrong** and we're feeling **sad**, we can say...

Help! God is **powerful** and can help us when we are in **trouble**.

Sorry! We all sometimes do bad things. Saying sorry clears the air and helps us to start over again.

"Do not worry about anything. But pray and ask God for everything you need. And when you pray, always give thanks." Philippians 4:6 (ICB)